My Favorite Bible Passages

_____

Other HarperSanFrancisco Books
by Norman Vincent Peale

My Favorite Quotations
My Christmas Treasury
My Inspirational Favorites
My Favorite Prayers
My Favorite Hymns

My Favorite Bible Passages

Norman Vincent Peale

A Giniger Book
published in association with

HarperSanFrancisco

A Division of HarperCollins*Publishers*

MY FAVORITE BIBLE PASSAGES. Copyright © 1995 by The Peale Foundation.
All rights reserved. Published in association with The K. S. Giniger
Company, Inc., 250 West 57th Street, New York, NY 10107.
Printed in the United States of America. No part of this book may
be used or reproduced in any manner whatsoever without written
permission except in the case of brief quotations embodied in
critical articles and reviews. For information address
HarperCollins Publishers,
10 East 53rd Street, New York, NY 10022.

FIRST EDITION

Library of Congress Cataloging-in-Publication Data
Bible. English, Authorized. Selections. 1995.
    My favorite Bible passages / Norman Vincent Peale. — 1st ed.
    ISBN 0-06-066452-5 (cloth)
    I. Peale, Norman Vincent. II. Title.
BS391.2.P43 1995
220.5'2036—dc20   95-3425
                                                           CIP

95 96 97 98 99 ❖ HAD 10 9 8 7 6 5 4 3 2 1

Contents

EDITOR'S NOTE

All Bible passages quoted are from the Authorized
King James Version of the Holy Bible, unless
the citation is followed by these designations:

(NIV) for *New International Version*

(TEV) for *Good News Bible: Today's English Version*

(RSV) for *Revised Standard Version*

(TLB) for *The Living Bible*

Thy word is a lamp unto my feet,
and a light unto my path.

Psalm 119:105

Introduction

In his more than seventy years of active ministry, Norman Vincent Peale delivered thousands of sermons and lectures, was heard by millions on radio and television, wrote hundreds of newspaper columns and magazine articles, and published forty-six books.

In all of these efforts to help people, he quoted extensively from the Bible, for his ministry was, indeed, Bible centered. In the very first sermon he preached, he took as his text: "I am come that they might have life, and that they might have it more abundantly" (John 10:10). He used this same text at the beginning of his ministry in every new church, and he expressed the hope that this would be the text for his last sermon. He quoted it more than any other verse throughout his career, and it became the cornerstone of his famous doctrine of "the power of positive thinking."

He had other favorite verses, particularly, "I can do all things through Christ which strengtheneth me"

(Philippians 4:13). Another of his favorites was Matthew 17:20: "If ye have faith as a grain of mustard seed, ye shall say unto this mountain, Remove hence to yonder place; and it shall remove: and nothing shall be impossible unto you."

Yet another favorite was: "Peace I leave with you, my peace I give unto you: not as the world giveth, give I unto you. Let not your heart be troubled, neither let it be afraid" (John 14:27).

He urged his listeners and readers to memorize the verses they found particularly meaningful and to repeat them over and over. He also encouraged writing these verses on pocket cards to carry or to put on mirrors where they could serve as constant daily reminders.

Norman particularly loved the story of the birth of Christ as told in the second chapter of the Gospel of Luke. This he always read to our family on Christmas Eve after we had finished decorating our tree. The story told that a baby had come into the world to show all of us the way to salvation and eternal life. His prayer following this reading expressed wonder, joy, reverence, and the promise of God's love for all.

On Christmas Eve 1993, Norman Vincent Peale was with me in his beloved Hill Farm home, surrounded by family. He was ninety-five years old, and his strength was weakening gradually. In a very beautiful, peaceful, and loving way the Lord let him "depart in peace."

I have chosen the Bible passages in this book from among the many used most often by Norman in his sermons, lectures, and writings. The brief introductory comments that precede each section of these favorite Bible passages have been taken from Norman's sermons and articles.

I appreciate the efficient work and sensitive care of my secretary, Sybil Light, in the preparation of this book. Kenneth Giniger, Norman's longtime editor and publisher, has been of tremendous help in finalizing this volume.

I hope that this selection of Norman Vincent Peale's favorite Bible passages will encourage you to read that "greatest of all books" and find favorites of your own.

Ruth Stafford Peale
The Hill Farm
Pawling, New York

One
The Power of Faith

The grass withereth,
the flower fadeth:
but the word of our God
shall stand for ever.

Isaiah 40:8

As an old hymn expresses it: "Change and decay in all around I see. / O thou who changest not, abide with me."

The years pass, loved ones go on ahead, papers yellow with age, the bloom of youth fades, white hair comes, changes follow one after the other, and we sadly say, "Things are not as they were."

But one thing never changes because it is truth, and truth is the same yesterday, today, and forever.

So, let us cleave to that which never fades, never withers—the word of God, which will stand forever.

We read in the Bible of the marvelous things Jesus did for people and rather wistfully wish that the same experiences might be ours. Through faith in Jesus Christ, they were able to accomplish the most astonishing achievements or were rescued from sad plights or gained tremendous new power over difficulties.

Rather sadly we ask, "Why cannot that happen to me?"

It can, and as proof I urge you to meditate upon this tremendous verse: Jesus Christ the same yesterday and today, and forever (Hebrews 13:8).

The simple truth stated here is that Jesus Christ never changes. He is an invariable factor in a variable world. He alone, of all people, is not a prisoner of his era. He is just the same now as he was when he walked the shores of Galilee. He has the same kindness, the same power to heal and change our lives. He is the same restorer of courage, the same transformer of our souls.

Anything he ever did for anyone throughout all history he can do for you. It all depends upon how completely you surrender yourself to him and how sincerely you believe.

We may never attain the enormous faith of the great saints, but what faith we do have must be the real thing. If we are completely dedicated to Christ, though our capacity for faith may not be great, if it is genuine, it releases power.

I suggest a daily exercise that has been helpful to many. Before arising each morning, voice this affirmation: "I believe, I believe, I believe." Then arise and believe your way through the day.

And Jacob went out from Beersheba, and went toward Haran.

And he lighted upon a certain place, and tarried there all night, because the sun was set; and he took of the stones of that place, and put them for his pillows, and lay down in that place to sleep.

And he dreamed, and behold a ladder set up on the earth, and the top of it reached to heaven: and behold the angels of God ascending and descending on it.

And, behold, the Lord stood above it, and said, I am the Lord God of Abraham thy father, and the God of Isaac: the land whereon thou liest, to thee will I give it, and to thy seed;

And thy seed shall be as the dust of the earth; and thou shalt spread abroad to the west, and to the east, and to the north, and to the south: and in thee and in thy seed shall all the families of the earth be blessed.

And behold, I am with thee, and will keep thee in all places wither thou goest, and will bring thee again into this land; for I will not leave thee, until I have done that which I have spoken to thee of.

And Jacob awaked out of his sleep, and he said, Surely the Lord is in this place; and I knew it not.

And he was afraid, and said, How dreadful is this place! this is none other but the house of God, and this is the gate of heaven.

And Jacob rose up early in the morning, and took the stone that he had put for his pillows, and set it up for a pillar, and poured oil upon the top of it.

And he called the name of that place Beth-el: but the name of that city was called Luz at the first.

And Jacob vowed a vow, saying, If God will be with me, and will keep me in this way that I go, and will give me bread to eat, and raiment to put on,

So that I come again to my father's house in peace; then shall the Lord be my God:

And this stone, which I have set for a pillar, shall be God's house: and of all that thou shalt give me I will surely give the tenth unto thee.

Genesis 28:10–22

Thou shalt have no other gods before me.

Thou shalt not make unto thee any graven image. . . .

Thou shalt not take the name of the Lord thy God in vain. . . .

Remember the sabbath day, to keep it holy. . . .

Honor thy father and thy mother: that thy days may be long upon the land which the Lord thy God giveth thee.

Thou shalt not kill.

Thou shalt not commit adultery.

Thou shalt not steal.

Thou shalt not bear false witness against thy neighbor.

Thou shalt not covet thy neighbor's house, thou shalt not covet thy neighbor's wife, nor his manservant, nor his maidservant, nor his ox, nor his ass, now any thing that is thy neighbor's.

Exodus 20:3–17

And I have filled him with the spirit of God, in wisdom, and in understanding, and in knowledge, and in all manner of workmanship.

Exodus 31:3

But if from thence thou shalt seek the Lord thy God, thou shalt find him, if thou seek him with all thy heart and with all thy soul.

Deuteronomy 4:29

The eternal God is thy refuge, and underneath are the everlasting arms.

Deuteronomy 33:27

Choose you this day whom ye will serve; . . . but as for me and my house, we will serve the Lord.

Joshua 24:15

The God of my rock; in him will I trust: he is my shield, and the horn of my salvation, my high tower, and my refuge, my saviour; thou savest me frcm violence.

2 Samuel 22:3

Though he slay me, yet will I trust in him.

Job 13:15

If thou return to the Almighty, thou shalt be built up.

Job 22:23

The Lord is my rock, and my fortress, and my deliverer; my God, my strength, in whom I will trust; my buckler, and the horn of my salvation, and my high tower.

Psalm 18:2

Our fathers trusted in thee; they trusted, and thou didst deliver them.

Psalm 22:4

The Lord is my light and my salvation; whom shall I fear? the Lord is the strength of my life; of whom shall I be afraid?

Psalm 27:1

O taste and see that the Lord is good: blessed is the man that trusteth in him.

Psalm 34:8

Commit thy way unto the Lord; trust also in him, and he shall bring it to pass.

Psalm 37:5

And he hath put a new song in my mouth, even praise unto our God: many shall see it, and fear, and shall trust in the Lord.

Psalm 40:3

Be still, and know that I am God.

Psalm 46:10

In God have I put my trust: I will not be afraid what man can do unto me.

Psalm 56:11

Truly my soul waiteth upon God: from him cometh my salvation.

Psalm 62:1

My soul, wait thou only upon God; for my expectation is from him.

Psalm 62:5

It is good for me to draw near to God: I have put my trust in the Lord God, that I may declare all thy works.

Psalm 73:28

Lord, thou hast been our dwelling place in all generations. Before the mountains were brought forth, or ever thou hadst formed the earth and the world, even from everlasting to everlasting, thou art God.

Psalm 90:1, 2

He that dwelleth in the secret place of the Most High shall abide under the shadow of the Almighty.

Psalm 91:1

Thy word is a lamp unto my feet, and a light unto my path.

Psalm 119:105

If I take the wings of the morning, and dwell in the uttermost parts of the sea;

Even there shall thy hand lead me, and thy right hand shall hold me.

Psalm 139:9, 10

The Lord is good to all: and his tender mercies are over all his works.

Psalm 145:9

Thy kingdom is an everlasting kingdom, and thy dominion endureth throughout all generations.

Psalm 145:13

For as he thinketh in his heart, so is he.

Proverbs 23:7

The Lord of hosts hath sworn, saying, Surely as I have thought, so shall it come to pass; and as I have purposed, so shall it stand.

Isaiah 14:24

Fear not; for I am with thee.

Isaiah 43:5

Incline your ear, and come unto me: hear, and your soul shall live; and I will make an everlasting covenant with you, even the sure mercies of David.

Behold, I have given him for a witness to the people, a leader and commander to the people.

Behold, thou shalt call a nation that thou knowest not, and nations that knew not thee shall run unto thee, because of the Lord thy God, and for the Holy One of Israel; for he hath glorified thee.

Seek ye the Lord while he may be found, call ye upon him while he is near:

Let the wicked forsake his way, and the unrighteous man his thoughts: and let him return unto the Lord, and he will have mercy upon him; and to our God, for he will abundantly pardon.

For my thoughts are not your thoughts, neither are your ways my ways, saith the Lord.

For as the heavens are higher than the earth, so are my ways higher than your ways, and my thoughts than your thoughts.

For as the rain cometh down, and the snow from heaven, and returneth not thither, but watereth the earth, and maketh it bring forth and bud, that it may give seed to the sower, and bread to the eater:

So shall my word be that goeth out of my mouth: it shall not return unto me void, but it shall accomplish that which I please, and it shall prosper in the thing whereto I sent it.

For ye shall go out with joy, and be led forth with peace: the mountains and the hills shall break forth before you into singing, and all the trees of the field shall clap their hands.

Isaiah 55:3–12

And the Lord shall guide thee continually, and satisfy thy soul in drought, and make fat thy bones: and thou shalt be like a watered garden, and like a spring of water, whose waters fail not.

Isaiah 58:11

And ye shall seek me, and find me, when ye shall search for me with all your heart.

Jeremiah 29:13

Behold, I am the Lord, the God of all flesh: is there any thing too hard for me?

Jeremiah 32:27

Although the fig tree shall not blossom, neither shall fruit be in the vines; the labor of the olive shall fail, and the fields shall yield no meat; the flock shall be cut off from the fold, and there shall be no herd in the stalls:

Yet I will rejoice in the Lord, I will joy in the God of my salvation.

The Lord God is my strength, . . . and he will make me to walk upon mine high places.

Habakkuk 3:17–18

And seeing the multitudes, he went up into a mountain: and when he was set, his disciples came unto him:

And he opened his mouth, and taught them, saying,

Blessed are the poor in spirit: for theirs is the kingdom of heaven.

Blessed are they that mourn: for they shall be comforted.

Blessed are the meek: for they shall inherit the earth.

Blessed are they which do hunger and thirst after righteousness: for they shall be filled.

Blessed are the merciful: for they shall obtain mercy.

Blessed are the pure in heart: for they shall see God.

Blessed are the peacemakers: for they shall be called the children of God.

Blessed are they which are persecuted for righteousness' sake: for theirs is the kingdom of heaven.

Blessed are ye, when men shall revile you, and persecute you, and shall say all manner of evil against you falsely, for my sake.

Rejoice, and be exceeding glad: for great is your reward in heaven: for so persecuted they the prophets which were before you.

Matthew 5:1–12

Behold the fowls of the air: for they sow not, neither do they reap, nor gather into barns; yet your heavenly Father feedeth them. Are ye not much better than they?

Which of you by taking thought can add one cubit unto his stature?

And why take ye thought for raiment? Consider the lilies of the field, how they grow; they toil not, neither do they spin:

And yet I say unto you, That even Solomon in all his glory was not arrayed like one of these.

Wherefore, if God so clothe the grass of the field, which to-day is, and to-morrow is cast into the oven, shall he not much more clothe you, O ye of little faith?

Therefore take no thought, saying, What shall we eat? or, What shall we drink? or, Wherewithal shall we be clothed?

(For after all these things do the Gentiles seek:) for your heavenly Father knoweth that ye have need of all these things.

But seek ye first the kingdom of God, and his righteousness; and all these things shall be added unto you.

Take therefore no thought for the morrow: for the morrow shall take thought for the things of itself. Sufficient unto the day is the evil thereof.

Matthew 6:26–34

Then said Jesus unto his disciples, If any man will come after me, let him deny himself, and take up his cross, and follow me.

Matthew 16:24

Verily I say unto you, Except ye be converted, and become as little children, ye shall not enter into the kingdom of heaven.

Matthew 18:3

With men this is impossible; but with God all things are possible.

Matthew 19:26

Verily I say unto you, If ye have faith, and doubt not, ye shall not only do this which is done to the fig tree, but also if ye shall say unto this mountain, Be thou removed, and be thou cast into the sea; it shall be done.

Matthew 21:21

Heaven and earth shall pass away, but my words shall not pass away.

Matthew 24:35

The time is fulfilled, and the kingdom of God is at hand: repent ye, and believe the gospel.

Mark 1:15

And Jesus said unto them, Come ye after me, and I will make you to become fishers of men.

Mark 1:17

Be not afraid, only believe.

Mark 5:36

If thou canst believe, all things are possible to him that believeth.

Mark 9:23

18

Lord, I believe; help thou mine unbelief.

Mark 9:24

And Jesus answering saith unto them, Have faith in God.

Mark 11:22

For verily I say unto you, That whosoever shall say unto this mountain, Be thou removed, and be thou cast into the sea; and shall not doubt in his heart, but shall believe that those things which he saith shall come to pass; he shall have whatsoever he saith.

Mark 11:23

Render unto Caesar the things that are Caesar's, and to God the things that are God's.

Mark 12:17

Blessed are they that hear the word of God, and keep it.

Luke 11:28

Fear not, little flock; for it is your Father's good pleasure to give you the kingdom.

Luke 12:32

The kingdom of God is within you.

Luke 17:21

Verily I say unto you, Whosoever shall not receive the kingdom of God as a little child shall in no wise enter therein.

Luke 18:17

The things which are impossible with men are possible with God.

Luke 18:27

In him was life; and the life was the light of men.

John 1:4

But as many as received him, to them gave he power to become the sons of God, even to them that believe on his name.

John 1:12

And of his fulness have all we received, and grace for grace.

John 1:16

Marvel not that I said unto thee, Ye must be born again.

John 3:7

For God so loved the world, that he gave his only begotten Son, that whosoever believeth in him should not perish, but have everlasting life.

John 3:16

Whosoever drinketh of the water that I shall give him shall never thirst; but the water that I shall give him shall be in him a well of water springing up unto everlasting life.

John 4:14

And Jesus said unto them, I am the bread of life: he that cometh to me shall never hunger; and he that believeth on me shall never thirst.

John 6:35

All that the Father giveth me shall come to me; and him that cometh to me I will in no wise cast out.

John 6:37

It is the Spirit that quickeneth; the flesh profiteth nothing: the words that I speak unto you, they are spirit, and they are life.

John 6:63

If any man thirst, let him come unto me, and drink.

He that believeth on me, as the Scripture hath said, out of his belly shall flow rivers of living water.

John 7:37–38

Then spake Jesus again unto them, saying, I am the light of the world: he that followeth me shall not walk in darkness, but shall have the light of life.

John 8:12

And ye shall know the truth, and the truth shall make you free.

John 8:32

I am the door: by me if any man enter in, he shall be saved, and shall go in and out, and find pasture.

John 10:9

My sheep hear my voice, and I know them, and they follow me:

And I give unto them eternal life; and they shall never perish, neither shall any man pluck them out of my hand.

John 10:27–28

I am the resurrection, and the life: he that believeth in me, though he were dead, yet shall he live:

And whosoever liveth and believeth in me shall never die.

John 11:25–26

If any man serve me, let him follow me; and where I am, there shall also my servant be: if any man serve me, him will my Father honor.

John 12:26

Jesus cried and said, He that believeth on me, believeth not on me, but on him that sent me.

And he that seeth me seeth him that sent me.

I am come a light into the world, that whosoever believeth on me should not abide in darkness.

John 12:44–46

I am the way, the truth, and the life: no man cometh unto the Father, but by me.

John 14:6

Verily, verily, I say unto you, He that believeth on me, the works that I do shall he do also; and greater works than these shall he do; believe I go unto my Father.

John 14:12

And whatsoever ye shall ask in my name, that will I do, that the Father may be glorified in the Son.

John 14:13

If ye shall ask any thing in my name, I will do it.

John 14:14

Peace I leave with you, my peace I give unto you: not as the world giveth, give I unto you. Let not your heart be troubled, neither let it be afraid.

John 14:27

If ye abide in me, and my words abide in you, ye shall ask what ye will, and it shall be done unto you.

John 15:7

Blessed are they that have not seen, and yet have believed.

John 20:29

Follow me.

John 21:19

Repent ye therefore, and be converted, that your sins may be blotted out, when the times of refreshing shall come from the presence of the Lord.

Acts 3:19

God that made the world and all things therein, seeing that he is Lord of heaven and earth, dwelleth not in temples made with hands;

Neither is worshipped with men's hands, as though he needed any thing, seeing he giveth to all life, and breath, and all things;

And hath made of one blood all nations of men for to dwell on all the face of the earth, and hath determined the times before appointed, and the bounds of their habitation;

That they should seek the Lord, if haply they might feel after him, and find him, though he be not far from every one of us:

For in him we live, and move, and have our being; as certain also of your own poets have said, For we are also his offspring.

Forasmuch then as we are the offspring of God, we ought not to think that the Godhead is like unto gold, or silver, or stone, graven by art and man's device.

And the times of this ignorance God winked at; but now commandeth all men every where to repent.

Acts 17:24–30

For in him we live, and move, and have our being.

Acts 17:28

For as many as are led by the Spirit of God, they are the sons of God.

Romans 8:14

All things work together for good to them that love God, to them who are the called according to his purpose.

Romans 8:28

If God be for us, who can be against us?

Romans 8:31

So then faith cometh by hearing, and hearing by the word of God.

Romans 10:17

Where the Spirit of the Lord is, there is liberty.

2 Corinthians 3:17

I am crucified with Christ: nevertheless I live; yet not I, but Christ liveth in me: and the life which I now live in the flesh I live by the faith of the Son of God, who loved me, and gave himself for me.

Galatians 2:20

In whom we have redemption through his blood, the forgiveness of sins, according to the riches of his grace.

Ephesians 1:7

Wherefore I also, after I heard of your faith in the Lord Jesus, and love unto all the saints, cease not to give thanks for you, making mention of you in my prayers.

Ephesians 1:15–16

That Christ may dwell in your hearts by faith; that ye, being rooted and grounded in love,

May be able to comprehend with all saints what is the breadth, and length, and depth, and height;

And to know the love of Christ, which passeth knowledge, that ye might be filled with all the fulness of God.

Ephesians 3:17–19

And be renewed in the spirit of your mind.

Ephesians 4:23

For ye were sometime darkness, but now are ye light in the Lord: walk as children of light.

Ephesians 5:8

And having this confidence, I know that I shall abide and continue with you all for your furtherance and joy of faith.

Philippians 1:25

Let this mind be in you, which was also in Christ Jesus.

Philippians 2:5

That ye might walk worthy of the Lord unto all pleasing, being fruitful in every good work, and increasing in the knowledge of God.

Colossians 1:10

Continue in the faith grounded and settled, and be not moved away from the hope of the gospel.

Colossians 1:23

Prove all things; hold fast that which is good.

1 Thessalonians 5:21

I have fought a good fight, I have finished my course, I have kept the faith.

2 Timothy 4:7

For we are made partakers of Christ, if we hold the beginning of our confidence steadfast unto the end.

Hebrews 3:14

That ye be not slothful, but followers of them who through faith and patience inherit the promises.

Hebrews 6:12

But without faith it is impossible to please him: for he that cometh to God must believe that he is, and that he is a rewarder of them that diligently seek him.

Hebrews 11:6

By faith Abraham . . . went out, not knowing whither he went. By faith he sojourned in the land of promise . . . for he looked for a city which hath foundations, whose builder and maker is God.

Hebrews 11:8–10

Wherefore, seeing we also are compassed about with so great a cloud of witnesses, let us lay aside every weight, and the sin which doth so easily beset us, and let us run with patience the race that is set before us,

Looking unto Jesus the author and finisher of our faith; who for the joy that was set before him endured the cross, despising the shame, and is set down at the right hand of the throne of God.

Hebrews 12:1–2

Jesus Christ the same yesterday, and today, and forever.

Hebrews 13:8

Being born again, not of corruptible seed, but of incorruptible, by the word of God, which liveth and abideth for ever.

1 Peter 1:23

He that hath the Son hath life; and he that hath not the Son of God hath not life.

1 John 5:12

Two
The Presence of Hope

_____

Why art thou cast down, O my soul?
and why art thou disquieted within me?
hope thou in God: for I shall yet praise
him, who is the health of my
countenance, and my God.

Psalm 42:11

Hope springs eternal in the human breast. And it is well that it does, for we cannot live without hope. But with it we can live successfully. It doesn't make any difference how much difficulty people experience; with hope they can still go forward.

Now it is a function of the Church of Jesus Christ to have a word, an answer, for human desperation, human depression, human suffering and woe. We have the word; or better still, three words: faith, hope, and love. Have that trinity in your mind, live by those shining words, and you have the secret of human life and life eternal. Faith, hope, and love. No matter what difficulties you may face, if you hope in God, the time will come when you will praise him for your victory and for his goodness.

This life is not easy. It is often fraught with pain and suffering. But hope gives you a lilting upthrust that takes you above the suffering. Storms sweep down upon human beings individually. And they sweep down over society. But if you hope in God and do the right things, according as you are given to know the right, storms pass after a while.

Nobody ought to go through life without developing a philosophy about storms. Storms are to toughen wood;

storms are to plow up the earth; storms are to test human beings; storms are hard, but one great thing about storms is that they always pass. And the things that are deeply rooted in the truth of Almighty God endure. So, if you are in harmony with God, you can have hope no matter how furious the storm.

O give thanks unto the Lord; for he is good; for his mercy endureth for ever.

1 Chronicles 16:34

My hope is in thee.

Psalm 39:7

For thou art my hope, O Lord God: thou art my trust from my youth.

Psalm 71:5

But I will hope continually, and will yet praise thee more and more.

Psalm 71:14

O Lord of hosts, blessed is the man that trusteth in thee.

Psalm 84:12

I wait for the Lord, my soul doth wait, and in his word do I hope.

Psalm 130:5

Hope deferred maketh the heart sick: but when the desire cometh, it is a tree of life.

Proverbs 13:12

The fear of the Lord tendeth to life: and he that hath it shall abide satisfied; he shall not be visited with evil.

Proverbs 19:23

Cast thy bread upon the waters: for thou shalt find it after many days.

Ecclesiastes 11:1

Come now, and let us reason together, saith the Lord: though your sins be as scarlet, they shall be as white as snow; though they be red like crimson, they shall be as wool.

Isaiah 1:18

It is good that a man should both hope and quietly wait for the salvation of the Lord.

Lamentations 3:26

Cast away from you all your transgressions, whereby ye have transgressed; and make you a new heart and a new spirit.

Ezekiel 18:31

The Lord will be the hope of his people.

Joel 3:16

And he spake many things unto them in parables, saying, Behold, a sower went forth to sow; and when he sowed, some seeds fell by the way side, and the fowls came and devoured them up: some fell upon stony places, where they had not much earth: and forthwith they sprung up, because they had no deepness of earth: and when the sun was up, they were scorched; and because they had no root, they withered away.

And some fell among thorns; and the thorns sprung up, and choked them: but others fell into good ground, and brought forth fruit, some a hundredfold, some sixtyfold, some thirtyfold.

Who hath ears to hear, let him hear . . .

Hear ye therefore the parable of the sower.

When any one heareth the word of the kingdom, and understandeth it not, then cometh the wicked one, and catcheth away that which was sown in his heart. This is he which received seed by the way side.

But he that received the seed into stony places, the same is he that heareth the word, and anon with joy receiveth it; yet hath he not root in himself, but dureth for a while: for when tribulation or persecution ariseth because of the word, by and by he is offended. He also that received seed among the thorns is he that heareth the word; and the care of this world, and the deceitfulness of riches, choke the word, and he becometh unfruitful. But he that received seed into the good ground is he that heareth the word, and understandeth it; which also beareth fruit, and bringeth forth, some a hundredfold, some sixty, some thirty.

Matthew 13:3–9, 18–23

For whosoever will save his life shall lose it: and whosoever will lose his life for my sake shall find it.

Matthew 16:25

41

And Jesus answered and said, Verily I say unto you, There is no man that hath left house, or brethren, or sisters, or father, or mother, or wife, or children, or lands, for my sake, and the gospel's, but he shall receive an hundredfold now in this time, houses, and brethren, and sisters, and mothers, and children, and lands, with persecutions; and in the world to come eternal life. But many that are first shall be last; and the last first.

Mark 10:29–31

And his mercy is on them that fear him from generation to generation.

Luke 1:50

Who against hope believe in hope . . .

Romans 4:18

We glory in tribulations also; knowing that tribulation worketh patience; and patience, experience; and experience, hope.

Romans 5:3–4

We are saved by hope.

Romans 8:24

For whatsoever things were written aforetime were written for our learning, that we through patience and comfort of the Scriptures might have hope.

Romans 15:4

Now the God of hope fill you with all joy and peace in believing.

Romans 15:13

And let us not be weary in well doing: for in due season we shall reap, if we faint not.

Galatians 6:9

To whom God would make known what is the riches of the glory of this mystery among the Gentiles; which is Christ in you, the hope of glory.

Colossians 1:27

Remembering without ceasing your ... patience of hope in our Lord Jesus Christ.

1 Thessalonians 1:3

Ye are all the children of light, and the children of the day: we are not of the night, nor of darkness.

1 Thessalonians 5:5

But let us, who are of the day, be sober, putting on the breastplate of faith and love; and for a helmet, the hope of salvation.

1 Thessalonians 5:8

Lay hold upon the hope set before us.

Hebrews 6:18

Which hope we have as an anchor of the soul, both sure and steadfast.

Hebrews 6:19

God resisteth the proud, but giveth grace unto the humble.

Submit yourselves therefore to God. Resist the devil, and he will flee from you.

Draw nigh to God, and he will draw nigh to you. Cleanse your hands, ye sinners; and purify your hearts, ye double-minded.

Humble yourselves in the sight of the Lord, and he shall lift you up.

James 4:6–8, 10

Blessed be the God and Father of our Lord Jesus Christ, which according to his abundant mercy hath begotten us again unto a lively hope by the resurrection of Jesus Christ from the dead.

1 Peter 1:3

But and if ye suffer for righteousness' sake, happy are ye: and be not afraid of their terror, neither be troubled;

But sanctify the Lord God in your hearts: and be ready always to give an answer to every man that asketh you a reason of the hope that is in you, with meekness and fear.

1 Peter 3:14, 15

Three
The Greatness of Love

If I speak in the tongues of men and of angels, but have not love, I am only a resounding gong or a clanging cymbal. If I have the gift of prophecy and can fathom all mysteries and all knowledge, and if I have a faith that can move mountains, but have not love, I am nothing. If I give all I possess to the poor and surrender my body to the flames, but have not love, I gain nothing.

Love is patient, love is kind. It does not envy, it does not boast, it is not proud. It is not rude, it is not self-seeking, it is not easily angered, it keeps no record of wrongs. Love does not delight in evil but rejoices with the truth. It always protects, always trusts, always hopes, always perseveres.

Love never fails. But where there are prophecies, they will cease; where there are tongues, they will be stilled; where there is knowledge, it will pass away. For we know in part and we prophesy in part, but when perfection comes, the imperfect disappears. When I was a child, I talked like a child, I thought like a child, I reasoned like a child. When I became a man, I put childish ways behind me. Now we see but a poor reflection as in a mirror; then we shall see face to face. Now I know in part; then I shall know fully, even as I am fully known. And now these three remain: faith, hope and love. But the greatest of these is love.

1 Corinthians 13:1–13 (NIV)

The Bible tells us that if we follow Jesus Christ, he will change us into the kind of people we want to be. So, if you want to have rapport and good relationships with other people, practice that suggestion. Love people and they will love you back.

There is a tremendous power in sending out love thoughts. We create around us, always, an aura or an atmosphere or a climate by the kind of thoughts we think. And people pick up that climate and respond to us accordingly.

There is a hard exercise, but one extremely important in developing a spiritual life. Resentment, ill will, the grudge, hate: these cause a sickness of the personality. Neither the mind nor the soul nor even the body can be fully healthy when such diseased attitudes are eating away at the life.

You can take steps to eradicate this spiritual illness and to gain a blessed healing. To do this, first relax. Resentment always tenses the being so the practice of relaxation, if continued long enough, will help you to let go of your ill will.

Now pass a series of love thoughts through your mind. Bring up one by one in your thoughts all the people you dearly love and thank God for them. This will tend toward conditioning your mind with love and make you amenable to the forgiveness discipline that you are now working to develop.

Next, shift to those whom you do not love, against whom you hold resentment. Try to think fair and kindly thoughts about them. This will no doubt come hard at first, but persistence will add to facility in such practice.

Slowly and thoughtfully, repeat the following verse: "But I say unto you, Love your enemies, bless them that curse you, do good to them that hate you, and pray for them which despitefully use you, and persecute you" (Matthew 5:44).

Now, name the person against whom you have the most dislike or greatest resentment, and bless him or her. By that, we mean, hold that person firmly in your consciousness and ask the Lord to bless him or her with good health, with prosperity, with every good thing.

You may want to tell yourself that this is dishonest, that you don't mean it. But that objection comes from your subconscious, where the hate has been lodged for so long. As you continue to bless and love this individual in your conscious mind, gradually your new attitude of love will penetrate the subconscious, ultimately displacing the hate thoughts. Then you will be released from your ill will and you will attain the wonderful spiritual achievement of forgiveness.

The greatest thing in this world is love, and never forget it. You are very foolish if you don't use this therapeutic methodology, because it was given to you to be used. It is the most powerful mental and spiritual influence known to the human race. And with it you can break down all kinds of barriers, all kinds of opposition, all kinds of failure and difficulty. The Bible says, "Little children, . . . love one another." That is one of the wisest statements ever made in the history of the human race.

Thou shalt not avenge, nor bear any grudge against the children of thy people, but thou shalt love thy neighbor as thyself: I am the Lord.

Leviticus 19:18

A soft answer turneth away wrath: but grievous words stir up anger.

Proverbs 15:1

When a man's ways please the Lord, he maketh even his enemies to be at peace with him.

Proverbs 16:7

A man that hath friends must show himself friendly: and there is a friend that sticketh closer than a brother.

Proverbs 18:24

For if they fall, the one will lift up his fellow: but woe to him that is alone when he falleth; for he hath not another to help him up.

Ecclesiastes 4:10

The Lord hath appeared of old unto me, saying, Yea, I have loved thee with an everlasting love: therefore with loving-kindness have I drawn thee.

Jeremiah 31:3

Love your enemies, bless them that curse you, do good to them that hate you, and pray for them which despitefully use you, and persecute you.

Matthew 5:44

For if ye forgive men their trespasses, your heavenly Father will also forgive you.

Matthew 6:14

For where your treasure is, there will your heart be also.

Matthew 6:21

Therefore all things whatsoever ye would that men should do to you, do ye even so to them: for this is the law and the prophets.

Matthew 7:12

If thy brother shall trespass against thee, go and tell him his fault between thee and him alone: if he shall hear thee, thou hast gained thy brother.

Matthew 18:15

Then came Peter to him, and said, Lord, how oft shall my brother sin against me, and I forgive him? till seven times?

Jesus saith unto him, I say not unto thee, Until seven times: but, Until seventy times seven.

Matthew 18:21–22

But it shall not be so among you: but whosoever will be great among you, let him be your minister; and whosoever will be chief among you, let him be your servant: even as the Son of man came not to be ministered unto, but to minister, and to give his life a ransom for many.

Matthew 20:26–28

Thou shalt love thy neighbor as thyself.

Matthew 22:39

But he that is greatest among you shall be your servant. And whosoever shall exalt himself shall be abased; and he that shall humble himself shall be exalted.

Matthew 23:11–12

Verily I say unto you, Inasmuch as ye have done it unto one of the least of these my brethren, ye have done it unto me.

Matthew 25:40

The first of all the commandments is, Hear, O Israel; The Lord our God is one Lord:

And thou shalt love the Lord thy God with all thy heart, and with all thy soul, and with all thy mind, and with all thy strength: this is the first commandment.

And the second is like, namely this, Thou shalt love thy neighbor as thyself. There is none other commandment greater than these.

Mark 12:29–31

But from the beginning of the creation God made them male and female. For this cause shall a man leave his father and mother, and cleave to his wife; and they twain shall be one flesh: so then they are no more twain, but one flesh. What therefore God hath joined together, let not man put asunder.

Mark 10:6–9

Give, and it shall be given unto you.

Luke 6:38

Whosoever shall receive this child in my name receiveth me; and whosoever shall receive me, receiveth him that sent me: for he that is least among you all, the same shall be great.

Luke 9:48

Thou shalt love the Lord thy God with all thy heart, and with all thy soul, and with all thy strength, and with all thy mind; and thy neighbor as thyself.

Luke 10:27

Father, forgive them; for they know not what they do.

Luke 23:34

A new commandment I give unto you, That ye love one another; as I have loved you, that ye also love one another.

By this shall all men know that ye are my disciples, if ye have love one to another.

John 13:34–35

If ye love me, keep my commandments.

John 14:15

As the Father hath loved me, so have I loved you: continue in my love.

John 15:9

This is my commandment, That ye love one another, as I have loved you.

John 15:12

Greater love hath no man than this, that a man lay down his life for his friends.

John 15:13

Be kindly affectioned one to another with brotherly love; in honor preferring one another.

Romans 12:10

If it be possible, as much as lieth in you, live peaceably with all men.

Romans 12:18

Owe no man any thing, but to love one another: for he that loveth another hath fulfilled the law.

Romans 13:8

For the love of Christ constraineth us.

2 Corinthians 4:14

For, brethren, ye have been called unto liberty; only use not liberty for an occasion to the flesh, but by love serve one another.

Galatians 5:13

But the fruit of the Spirit is love, joy, peace, long-suffering, gentleness, goodness, faith,
Meekness, temperance: against such there is no law.

Galatians 5:22–23

If we live in the Spirit, let us also walk in the Spirit.

Let us not be desirous of vainglory, provoking one another, envying one another.

Brethren, if a man be overtaken in a fault, ye which are spiritual, restore such a one in the spirit of meekness; considering thyself, lest thou also be tempted.

Bear ye one another's burdens, and so fulfill the law of Christ.

Galatians 5:25–6:2

Be ye angry, and sin not: let not the sun go down upon your wrath.

Ephesians 4:26

And be ye kind one to another, tender-hearted, forgiving one another, even as God for Christ's sake hath forgiven you.

Ephesians 4:32

Walk in love. . . . Walk as children of light.

Ephesians 5:2, 8

Let nothing be done through strife or vainglory; but in lowliness of mind let each esteem other better than themselves.

Philippians 2:3

Put on therefore . . . mercies, kindness, humbleness of mind, meekness, longsuffering;
Forbearing one another, and forgiving one another, if any man have a quarrel against any: even as Christ forgave you, so also do ye.

Colossians 3:12–13

Let brotherly love continue.

Hebrews 13:1

Finally, be ye all of one mind, having compassion one of another; love as brethren, be pitiful, be courteous.

1 Peter 3:8

My little children, let us not love in word, neither in tongue; but in deed and in truth.

And this is his commandment, That we should believe on the name of his Son Jesus Christ, and love one another, as he gave us commandment.

1 John 3:18, 23

Let us love one another, for love is of God.

1 John 4:7

He that loveth not, knoweth not God; for God is love.

1 John 4:8

There is no fear in love; but perfect love casteth out fear: because fear hath torment. He that feareth is not made perfect in love.

1 John 4:18

We love him, because he first loved us.

If a man say, I love God, and hateth his brother, he is a liar: for he that loveth not his brother whom he hath seen, how can he love God whom he hath not seen?

And this commandment have we from him, That he who loveth God love his brother also.

1 John 4:19–21

Four
The Promise of Prayer

---

*And the Lord spake unto
Moses face to face, as a man
speaketh unto his friend.*

Exodus 33:11

Effective praying is talking naturally, honestly, sincerely, and in a straightforward manner to God. Do not feel that you must clothe your speech in stilted, traditional language. The language God wants to hear is that of the humble, contrite heart.

Many people feel that they have lost contact with God. But he is our best friend. Believe in God and really learn to know and love him. Set aside a few minutes each day simply to talk to him. Thank him for the blessings he has given you, and tell him your desires and hurts and problems while expressing your willingness to accept his will. He may give you more blessings than you ask for. That is a loving way he has.

Remember that God loves you so very much. He will always be close by to help you. He will never leave you.

To pray successfully, you must employ affirmation and visualization. Form a picture in your mind, not of lack or denial or frustration or illness, but of prosperity, abundance, attainment, health. Always remember you will receive as a result of prayer exactly what you think, not what you say. If you pray for achievement but think defeat, your words are idle because your heart has already accepted defeat.

Therefore, practice believing that even as you pray you are receiving God's boundless blessings, and they will come to you.

If you are not getting answers to your prayers, check yourself very thoroughly and honestly as to whether you have resentments in your mind.

Spiritual power cannot pass through a personality where resentment exists. Hate is a nonconductor of spiritual energy.

I suggest that every time you pray, you add this phrase, "Lord, take from my thought all ill will, grudges, hates, jealousies." Then practice casting these things from your thoughts.

To get answers to your prayers, keep praying. Don't stop, go deeper; just keep on praying, until prayer wells up in full measure within you, until you really mean your prayers with all your heart. Wrestle with your problem in prayer. Really go after an answer, strongly believing you are going to get it. Ask . . . knock . . . seek. The Lord himself advises us to do so.

You can have complete confidence in the Lord and in his promises. If you have his mind and talk his language, possess his spirit, identify with his purposes, have his love in your heart, are in his will, he will always hear you.

And God *does* always answer sincere prayer. He answers in three ways: (1) yes, (2) no, (3) wait awhile. And every answer, whatever it may be, is for our good as long as we are in his will.

> When thou hast eaten and art full, then thou shalt bless the Lord thy God for the good land which he hath given thee. Beware that thou forget not the Lord thy God, in not keeping his commandments, and his judgments, and his statues, which I command thee this day.
>
> *Deuteronomy 8:10, 11*

> Stand every morning to thank and praise the Lord, and likewise at evening.
>
> *1 Chronicles 23:30*

If my people, which are called by my name, shall humble themselves, and pray, and seek my face, and turn from their wicked ways; then will I hear from heaven, and will forgive their sin, and will heal their land.

2 Chronicles 7:14

My voice shalt thou hear in the morning, O Lord; in the morning will I direct my prayer unto thee, and will look up.

Psalm 5:3

I sought the Lord, and he heard me, and delivered me from all my fears.

Psalm 34:4

Evening, and morning, and at noon, will I pray, and cry aloud: and he shall hear my voice.

Psalm 55:17

What time I am afraid, I will trust in thee.

When I cry unto thee, then shall mine enemies turn back: this I know; for God is for me.

Psalm 56:3, 9

Because thy loving-kindness is better than life, my lips shall praise thee.

Psalm 63:3

Let the people praise thee, O God; let all the people praise thee.

Then shall the earth yield her increase; and God, even our own God, shall bless us.

Psalm 67:5–6

Unto thee, O God, do we give thanks, unto thee do we give thanks: for that thy name is near thy wondrous works declare.

Psalm 75:1

It is a good thing to give thanks unto the Lord, and to sing praises unto thy name, O Most High.

Psalm 92:1

Praise ye the Lord. O give thanks unto the Lord; for he is good: for his mercy endureth for ever.

Psalm 106:1

I will praise thee; for I am fearfully and wonderfully made: marvelous are thy works; and that my soul knoweth right well.

Psalm 139:14

The Lord is near to all who call upon him, to all who call upon him in truth.

Psalm 145:18

This is the refreshing.

Isaiah 28:12

And it shall come to pass, that before they call, I will answer; and while they are yet speaking, I will hear.

Isaiah 65:24

Call unto me, and I will answer thee, and show thee great and mighty things, which thou knowest not.

Jeremiah 33:3

But when ye pray, use not vain repetitions, as the heathen do: for they think that they shall be heard for their much speaking.

Be not ye therefore like unto them: for your Father knoweth what things ye have need of, before ye ask them.

Matthew 6:7–8

Ask, and it shall be given you; seek, and ye shall find; knock, and it shall be opened unto you.

Matthew 7:7

Again I say unto you, That if two of you shall agree on earth as touching any thing that they shall ask, it shall be done for them of my Father which is in heaven.

For where two or three are gathered together in my name, there am I in the midst of them.

Matthew 18:19–20

And all things, whatsoever ye shall ask in prayer, believing, ye shall receive.

Matthew 21:22

And Jesus answering saith unto them, Have faith in God.

For verily I say unto you, That whosoever shall say unto this mountain, Be thou removed, and be thou cast into the sea; and shall not doubt in his heart, but shall believe that those things which he saith shall come to pass; he shall have whatsoever he saith.

Therefore I say unto you, What things soever ye desire, when ye pray, believe that ye receive them, and ye shall have them.

And when ye stand praying, forgive, if ye have aught against any; that your Father also which is in heaven may forgive you your trespasses.

But if ye do not forgive, neither will your father which is in heaven forgive your trespasses.

Mark 11:22–26

One of his disciples said unto him, Lord, teach us to pray. . . .

And he said unto them, When ye pray, say, Our Father which art in heaven, Hallowed be thy name. Thy kingdom come. Thy will be done, as in heaven, so in earth.

Give us day by day our daily bread.

And forgive us our sins; for we also forgive everyone that is indebted to us. And lead us not into temptation; but deliver us from evil.

Luke 11:1–4

And I say unto you, Ask, and it shall be given you; seek, and ye shall find; knock and it shall be opened unto you.

For every one that asketh receiveth; and he that seeketh findeth; and to him that knocketh it shall be opened.

Luke 11:9–10

Men ought always to pray.

Luke 18:1

God is a Spirit: and they that worship him must worship him in spirit and in truth.

John 4:24

Giving thanks always for all things unto God and the Father in the name of our Lord Jesus Christ.

Ephesians 5:20

Pray without ceasing.

1 Thessalonians 5:17

In every thing give thanks: for this is the will of God in Christ Jesus concerning you.

1 Thessalonians 5:18

If any of you lack wisdom, let him ask of God, that giveth to all men liberally, and upbraideth not; and it shall be given him.

But let him ask in faith, nothing wavering: for he that wavereth is like a wave of the sea driven with the wind and tossed.

James 1:5, 6

But ye are a chosen generation, a royal priesthood, a holy nation, a peculiar people; that ye should show forth the praises of him who hath called you out of darkness into his marvelous light.

1 Peter 2:9

Casting all your care upon him; for he careth for you.

1 Peter 5:7

And this is the confidence that we have in him, that, if we ask any thing according to his will, he heareth us.

1 John 5:14

Five

The Source of Strength

I can do all things through Christ which strengtheneth me. . . . But my God shall supply all your need according to his riches in glory by Christ Jesus.

Philippians 4:13, 19

This passage is an antidote for every feeling of defeat. If you feel downed by situations and the going is hard, this statement will remind you that you do not need to depend upon your own strength entirely, but that Christ is with you and is *now* giving you all the help you need.

Teach yourself to believe that through Christ's help you *can* do all things. As you continue this affirmation, you will actually experience Christ's help. You will find yourself meeting problems with new mental force. You will carry heavy burdens with ease. Your new "lifting" power will amaze you.

God is the source of all energy: in the sun, in plants, and in people. Through the channel of spiritual thought, he will pour new energy and strength into you. You will feel it physically, emotionally, and mentally.

Conceive of our Lord as touching you. Affirm that he is sending into your being his illimitable strength.

God makes a most important promise to you. No matter how awesome your problems, you need have no fear. Certainly you are not to let anything dismay you, for God says he will strengthen and help you. In fact, he promises he will hold you up and make you adequate for any situation.

Accept this great fact. Hold this strongly in your consciousness until it sends its ruggedness throughout your entire life.

Scarcely any joy equals the realization that you have it in you to meet all your responsibilities. This consciousness contributes immeasurably to high spirit and happiness. It is quite difficult, on the contrary, to face each day with a sense of inability and weakness. With such an attitude, life seems too much, and profound discouragement sets in.

Spirit goes out of you when overwhelmed and defeated. Get firmly based on spiritual understanding, on faith and goodness. Then nothing can defeat you.

Live by the saying of Jesus Christ and become like that wise man who built his house upon rock and against which the storms beat in vain: unshakable. You can have an inner serenity, strength, and courage that defies all the storms of life. Christ makes you strong. You can be undefeatable.

The greatest fact of all is that God is with us. We are not alone. He will never leave or forsake us but will protect, guide, and comfort us at any time, anywhere.

When the going is hard and you feel insecure and maybe fearful, just say this wonderful promise and remind yourself that he is always with you—always.

The Lord, he it is that doth go before thee; he will be with thee, he will not fail thee, neither forsake thee: fear not, neither be dismayed.

Deuteronomy 31:8

I will be with thee: I will not fail thee, nor forsake thee.

Joshua 1:5

Be strong and of a good courage; be not afraid, neither be thou dismayed: for the Lord thy God is with thee whithersoever thou goest.

Joshua 1:9

God is my strength and power; and he maketh my way perfect.

2 Samuel 22:33

Believe in the Lord your God, so shall ye be established.

2 Chronicles 20:20

The joy of the Lord is your strength.

Nehemiah 8:10

Blessed is the man that walketh not in the counsel of the ungodly, nor standeth in the way of sinners, nor sitteth in the seat of the scornful.

But his delight is in the law of the Lord; and in his law doth he meditate day and night.

And he shall be like a tree planted by the rivers of water, that bringeth forth his fruit in his season; his leaf also shall not wither; and whatsoever he doeth shall prosper.

The ungodly are not so: but are like the chaff which the wind driveth away.

Therefore the ungodly shall not stand in the judgment, nor sinners in the congregation of the righteous.

For the Lord knoweth the way of the righteous: but the way of the ungodly shall perish.

Psalm 1

When I consider thy heavens, the work of thy fingers, the moon and the stars, which thou hast ordained;

What is man, that thou art mindful of him? and the son of man, that thou visitest him?

For thou hast made him a little lower than the angels, and hast crowned him with glory and honor.

Psalm 8:3–5

For by thee I have run through a troop; and by my God have I leaped over a wall.

Psalm 18:29

Though a host should encamp against me, my heart shall not fear: though war should rise against me, in this will I be confident.

Psalm 27:3

Delight thyself also in the Lord; and he shall give thee the desires of thine heart.

Psalm 37:4

Offer unto God thanksgiving; and pay thy vows unto the Most High:
And call upon me in the day of trouble: I will deliver thee, and thou shalt glorify me.

Psalm 50:14–15

But I will sing of thy power; yea, I will sing aloud of thy mercy in the morning: for thou hast been my defense and refuge in the day of my trouble.
Unto thee, O my strength, will I sing: for God is my defense, and the God of my mercy.

Psalm 59:16–17

Hear my cry, O God; attend unto my prayer.
From the end of the earth will I cry unto thee, when my heart is overwhelmed: lead me to the rock that is higher than I.

For thou has been a shelter for me, and a strong tower from the enemy.

I will abide in thy tabernacle for ever: I will trust in the covert of thy wings.

Psalm 61:1–4

Counsel is mine, and sound wisdom: I am understanding; I have strength.

Proverbs 8:14

In the fear of the Lord is strong confidence: and his children shall have a place of refuge.

Proverbs 14:26

Behold, God is my salvation; I will trust, and not be afraid: for the Lord Jehovah is my strength and my song; he also is become my salvation.

Isaiah 12:2

In quietness and in confidence shall be your strength.

Isaiah 30:15

Strengthen ye the weak hands, and confirm the feeble knees.

Say to them that are of a fearful heart, Be strong, fear not: behold, your God will come with vengeance, even God with a recompense; he will come and save you.

Isaiah 35:3–4

Hast thou not known? hast thou not heard, that the everlasting God, the Lord, the Creator of the ends of the earth, fainteth not, neither is weary? there is no searching of his understanding.

He giveth power to the faint; and to them that have no might he increaseth strength.

Even the youths shall faint and be weary, and the young men shall utterly fall:

But they that wait upon the Lord shall renew their strength; they shall mount up with wings as eagles; they shall run, and not be weary; and they shall walk, and not faint.

Isaiah 40:28–31

Fear thou not; for I am with thee: be not dismayed; for I am thy God: I will strengthen thee; yea, I will help thee; yea, I will uphold thee with the right hand of my righteousness.

Isaiah 41:10

For I the Lord thy God will hold thy right hand, saying unto thee, Fear not; I will help thee.

Isaiah 41:13

The people that do know their God shall be strong, and do exploits.

Daniel 11:32

Let the weak say, I am strong.

Joel 3:10

Truly I am full of power by the Spirit of the Lord.

Micah 3:8

Therefore whosoever heareth these sayings of mine, and doeth them, I will liken him unto a wise man, which built his house upon a rock:

And the rain descended, and the floods came, and the winds blew, and beat upon that house; and it fell not: for it was founded upon a rock.

And every one that heareth these saying of mine, and doeth them not, shall be likened unto a foolish man, which built his house upon the sand:

And the rain descended, and the floods came, and the winds blew, and beat upon that house; and it fell: and great was the fall of it.

Matthew 7:24–27

Behold, I give unto you power to tread on serpents and scorpions, and over all the power of the enemy; and nothing shall by any means hurt you.

Luke 10:19

The things which are impossible with men are possible with God.

Luke 18:27

But when ye shall hear of wars and commotions, be not terrified: for these things must first come to pass; but the end is not by and by.

Luke 21:9

I am not alone, because the Father is with me.

John 16:32

Ye shall receive power, after that the Holy Ghost is come upon you.

Acts 1:8

Walk in newness of life.

Romans 6:4

There hath no temptation taken you but such as is common to man: but God is faithful, who will not suffer you to be tempted above that ye are able; but will with the temptation also make a way to escape, that ye may be able to bear it.

1 Corinthians 10:13

But thanks be to God, which giveth us the victory through our Lord Jesus Christ.

1 Corinthians 15:57

Watch ye, stand fast in the faith, quit you like men, be strong.

1 Corinthians 16:13

Therefore, seeing we have this ministry, as we have received mercy, we faint not.

2 Corinthians 4:1

That he would grant you, according to the riches of his glory, to be strengthened with might by his Spirit in the inner man.

Ephesians 3:16

Now unto him that is able to do exceeding abundantly above all that we ask or think, according to the power that worketh in us.

Ephesians 3:20

Be strong in the Lord, and in the power of his might.

Ephesians 6:10

Put on the whole armor of God, that ye may be able to stand against the wiles of the devil.

For we wrestle not against flesh and blood, but against principalities, against powers, against the rulers of the darkness of this world, against spiritual wickedness in high places.

Wherefore take unto you the whole armor of God, that ye may be able to withstand in the evil day, and having done all, to stand.

Stand therefore, having your loins girt about with truth, and having on the breastplate of righteousness;

And your feet shod with the preparation of the gospel of peace;

Above all, taking the shield of faith, wherewith ye shall be able to quench all the fiery darts of the wicked.

And take the helmet of salvation, and the sword of the spirit, which is the word of God.

Ephesians 6:11–17

I can do all things through Christ which strengtheneth me.

Philippians 4:13

But my God shall supply all your need according to his riches in glory by Christ Jesus.

Philippians 4:19

For this cause we also, since the day we heard it, do not cease to pray for you, and to desire that ye might be filled with the knowledge of his will in all wisdom and spiritual understanding;
Strengthened with all might, according to his glorious power, unto all patience and long-suffering with joyfulness.

Colossians 1:9, 11

Cast not away therefore your confidence, which hath great recompense of reward.

Hebrews 10:35

Who through faith subdued kingdoms.

Hebrews 11:33

Out of weakness were made strong.

Hebrews 11:34

The Lord is my helper, and I will not fear what man shall do unto me.

Hebrews 13:6

Humble yourselves therefore, under the mighty hand of God, that he may exalt you in due time.

1 Peter 5:6

Whatsoever is born of God overcometh the world.

1 John 5:4

Behold, I have set before thee an open door, and no man can shut it: for thou hast a little strength, and hast kept my word, and hast not denied my name.

Revelation 3:8

He that overcometh shall inherit all things; and I will be his God, and he shall be my son.

Revelation 21:7

Six

The Secret of Peace
and Happiness

---

*Come unto me, all ye that labor and
are heavy laden, and I will give you rest.
Take my yoke upon you, and learn of me;
for I am meek and lowly in heart: and
ye shall find rest unto your souls. For my
yoke is easy, and my burden is light.*

Matthew 11:28–30

Perhaps the strain and burden of life have made you tired. If so, maybe you are carrying life too heavily.

Primarily, we do not get tired in our muscles but in our minds. We develop that "I'm swamped" feeling.

Allow this text to dissolve in your thoughts as a kind of spiritual lozenge. As you turn to Jesus in your thoughts, he will give you rest. And how does he do that? One way is by showing you how to work.

"Learn of me," he says. In other words, work by my method. "My yoke is easy, and my burden is light." That is to say, easy does it. Don't strain, don't tug, relax. Do one job at a time using the light touch, the easy stroke.

Do you have life in all its fullness? If you haven't, that is a shame. But something can happen to you right now that will make you so enthusiastic and so excited that you will have life in all of its fullness.

You may ask, "How do I get that?" One important thing in getting life of this quality is to turn your life over to God and let him do with it what he wants to do. You see, when we try to run our own lives, we so often mess them up. Or if we don't really mess them up, we do not release them to their fullest potential and possibility.

So the secret is to put your life in God's hands and tell him you want him to take charge, to guide and direct you. And he will do it in the most unexpected manner.

Jesus gets the biggest men among us. Jesus gets the greatest women among us. Jesus gets the greatest minds among us, because nobody has ever been able to think as he did. He is the amazement and the astonishment of the scholars of all time because he is able to take the simple truth and make it winsome and reasonable.

Nobody but Jesus has ever been able to change human beings. Over many years, people in all walks of life have been changed: failures, wicked people, mixed-up people, unhappy people, defeated people. They come into a glorious house of God and find ministers who have found Jesus and are able to lead them up to Jesus. Then they become enthusiastic. They become excited. Wonders start happening in their lives.

Something wonderful can happen to you today. Believe it and accept it.

I met a joy-motivated businessman some years ago in the South. Struck by his happy manner and noting the obviously high regard in which he was held by everyone,

I asked him the secret of his refreshing enjoyment of life. For him every day seemed a delightful experience. In reply to my question he handed me a small box containing a beautifully framed and artistic card on which were embossed the words "What would Jesus do?"

He explained that he had experienced a series of failures resulting in unhappiness, or, as he admitted, perhaps his failure pattern had resulted from his unhappy attitude. He became so miserable that finally he consulted his pastor, who proved to be a very wise guide. The pastor pointed out that Jesus had deep inner peace and joy despite everything he faced and suggested to the man that the surest way to have the same inner peace and joy would be to live and think and act as Jesus did. "In every situation just ask, 'What would Jesus do?' and then do that," the pastor advised.

The man was impressed. He followed the advice, and it changed his life so much that he had the words embossed on cards and framed. At the time I met him he had given over three thousand of these to men and women who asked his secret for having a good day every day.

We become low spirited when we weakly give into temptation. Such defeat dulls the spirit, subtracting that keen sense of happiness one enjoys when in full control.

The way to overcome temptation is: sincerely want God's help. Earnestly ask for it; believe you have it; act as God wants you to. This will make you happy and high spirited.

Acquaint now thyself with him, and be at peace: thereby good shall come unto thee.

Job 22:21

When he giveth quietness, who then can make trouble?

Job 34:29

Thou wilt show me the path of life: in thy presence is fulness of joy; at thy right hand there are pleasures for evermore.

Psalm 16:11

I have been young, and now am old; yet have I not seen the righteous forsaken, nor his seed begging bread.

Psalm 37:25

He formed the mountains by his mighty strength. He quiets the raging oceans and all the world's clamor. In the farthest corners of the earth the glorious acts of God shall startle everyone. The dawn and sunset shout for joy! He waters the earth to make it fertile. The rivers of God will not run dry! He preparest the earth for his people and sends them rich harvests of grain. He waters the furrows with abundant rain. Showers soften the earth, melting the clods and causing seeds to sprout across the land. Then he crowns it all with green, lush pastures in the wilderness; hillsides blossom with joy. The pastures are filled with flocks of sheep, and the valleys are carpeted with grain. All the world shouts with joy, and sings.

Psalm 65:6–13 (TLB)

O satisfy us early with thy mercy; that we may rejoice and be glad all our days.

Psalm 90:14

This is the day which the Lord hath made; we will rejoice and be glad in it.

Psalm 118:24

Great peace have they which love thy law: and nothing shall offend them.

Psalm 119:165

For thou shalt eat the labor of thine hands: happy shalt thou be, and it shall be well with thee.

Psalm 128:2

Happy is the man that findeth wisdom, and the man that getteth understanding.

Proverbs 3:13

The hope of the righteous shall be gladness: but the expectation of the wicked shall perish.

Proverbs 10:28

All the days of the afflicted are evil: but he that is of a merry heart hath a continual feast.

Proverbs 15:15

He that handleth a matter wisely shall find good: and whoso trusteth in the Lord, happy is he.

Proverbs 16:20

Thou wilt keep him in perfect peace, whose mind is stayed on thee: because he trusteth in thee.

Isaiah 26:3

For ye shall go out with joy, and be led forth with peace: the mountains and the hills shall break forth before you into singing, and all the trees of the field shall clap their hands.

Isaiah 55:12

Thy words were found, and I did eat them; and thy word was unto me the joy and rejoicing of mine heart: for I am called by thy name, O Lord God of hosts.

Jeremiah 15:16

Bring ye all the tithes into the storehouse, that there may be meat in mine house, and prove me now herewith, saith the Lord of hosts, if I will not open you the windows of heaven, and pour you out a blessing, that there shall not be room enough to receive it.

Malachi 3:10

Be ye therefore perfect, even as our Father which is in heaven is perfect.

Matthew 5:48

Be of good cheer; it is I; be not afraid.

Matthew 14:27

For they all saw him, and were troubled. And immediately he talked with them, and saith unto them, Be of good cheer: it is I; be not afraid.

Mark 6:50

Likewise, I say unto you, there is joy in the presence of the angels of God over one sinner that repenteth.

Luke 15:10

If ye know these things, happy are ye if ye do them.

John 13:17

These things have I spoken unto you, that my joy might remain in you, and that your joy might be full.

John 15:11

Hitherto have ye asked nothing in my name: ask, and ye shall receive, that your joy may be full.

John 16:24

Peace be unto you.

John 20:19

Thou has made known to me the ways of life; thou shalt make me full of joy with thy countenance.

Acts 2:28

To be spiritually minded is life and peace.

Romans 8:6

Rejoice in the Lord always: and again I say, Rejoice.

Philippians 4:4

Finally, brethren, whatsoever things are true, whatsoever things are honest, whatsoever things are just, whatsoever things are pure, whatsoever things are lovely, whatsoever things are of good report; if there be any virtue, and if there be any praise, think on these things.

Those things, which ye have both learned, and received, and heard, and seen in me, do: and the God of peace shall be with you.

Philippians 4:8–9

I have learned, in whatsoever state I am, therewith to be content.

I know both how to be abased, and I know how to abound: every where and in all things I am instructed both to be full and to be hungry, both to abound and to suffer need.

Philippians 4:11, 12

And let the peace of God rule in your hearts, to the which also ye are called in one body; and be ye thankful.

Colossians 3:15

And we beseech you, brethren, to know them which labor among you, and are over you in the Lord, and admonish you;

And to esteem them very highly in love for their work's sake. And be at peace among yourselves.

1 Thessalonians 5:12, 13

Rejoice evermore.

1 Thessalonians 5:16

I exhort therefore, that, first of all, supplications, prayers, intercessions, and giving of thanks, be made for all men; for kings, and for all that are in authority; that we may lead a quiet and peaceable life in all godliness and honesty.

1 Timothy 2:2

Behold, we count them happy which endure. Ye have heard of the patience of Job, and have seen the end of the Lord; that the Lord is very pitiful, and of tender mercy.

James 5:11

Believing, ye rejoice with joy unspeakable and full of glory.

1 Peter 1:8

For he that will love life, and see good days, let him refrain his tongue from evil, and his lips that they speak no guile:

Let him eschew evil, and do good; let him seek peace, and ensue it.

1 Peter 3:10–11

Seven
The Wonder of Healing

---

*And the whole multitude sought to touch
him: for there went virtue out of him,
and healed them all.*

Luke 6:19

The power of Jesus Christ is very skillful. "God moves in a mysterious way / His wonders to perform, . . ." said William Cowper, the English poet. No wonder the multitudes two thousand years ago sought to touch him and power came out of him and healed them all. And today, twenty centuries later, he is still the greatest healer among all the great healers of the world.

A great French physician once said, "I treat the patient, but God alone can heal him." And I know a surgeon who, when he has completed an operation and is washing up, says, "Now it's up to you." So Jesus Christ is still the supreme master of human illness.

An important factor in the matter is this: Good emotions make us well; bad emotions make us sick. What are bad emotions? Anger, hate, resentment, fear. These make us sick. And what are good emotions? Faith, joy, happiness, love. These tend to make us well. Dr. John A. Schindler, in his book titled *How to Live 365 Days a Year*, says, "The Ochsner Clinic in New Orleans published a paper which stated that 74 percent of 500 consecutive patients admitted to the department handling gastrointestinal diseases were found to be suffering from emotionally induced illness." Imagine, all those people made ill because of bad emotions. That is not from the pulpit; that is from a clinic.

Another physician, who ran a great clinic in Cleveland, said years ago that three things cause more human sickness than anything else: fear, anger, and guilt. They produce weariness and lack of vitality.

The house of God, ordinarily called a church, is actually a spiritual hospital to which people come with diseases in their bodies or diseases in their minds or diseases in their souls. Here the Great Physician touches them and makes them well. I really do believe this. "And the whole multitude sought to touch him: for there went virtue out of him, and healed them all."

From disorder in our lives and from bad emotions, as contrasted with good emotions, we develop illness. But illness can be cured by the mysterious healing power of faith. I don't pretend to understand this power. I only witness to the fact that it exists and performs wonders.

To experience his healing power, yield yourself to him willingly. Make the first move, however timidly. He will respond with the miraculous touch that makes you whole in body, mind, and spirit. How your spirits rise as you gain a deep inner sense of wholeness!

Take the medicine of faith. You take it in through the eye; you read the Bible. The great words you read cause a reflection on the retina of the eye. These words form into an idea, the most powerful combination of words in all the world. And this idea seeks out and finds in the brain the center of the infection and heals it!

When illness comes, use prayers of faith, visualizing yourself as getting well and becoming whole. Such prayers will attune your mind to God and permit his healing power to come into your body and mind. You will discover that the prayer of faith is one of the most powerful influences in opening your spirit to the healing hands of your doctor and of God.

If you are not healed right away, do not worry. God does things in his own time, which is often different from ours. He has not forgotten you. Whatever his plan may be, trust him implicitly. He will give you health and strength.

God, our creator, is also our recreator. So long as we are in unbroken contact with God, the life force continues strong within us. But, having the power of choice, we may choose life or we may actually turn it off, depending upon how well we maintain spiritual contact.

When the life flow from God is reduced, we run down in energy, health, and power. But the recreative process or life renewal restores power and energy, and it is not complicated. Simply love God, obey his voice, cleave unto him. Then he will truly be "thy life, and the length of thy days."

I am the Lord that healeth thee.

Exodus 15:26

My presence shall go with thee, and I will give thee rest.

Exodus 33:14

I have set before you life and death, blessing and cursing: therefore choose life, that both thou and thy seed may live.

Deuteronomy 30:19

Behold, happy is the man whom God correcteth: therefore despise not thou the chastening of the Almighty:

For he maketh sore, and bindeth up: he woundeth, and his hands make whole.

Job 5:17, 18

When men are cast down, then thou shalt say, There is lifting up.

Job 22:29

I laid me down and slept; I awaked; for the Lord sustained me.

Psalm 3:5

Have mercy upon me, O Lord; for I am weak: O Lord,
heal me; for my bones are vexed.

Psalm 6:2

They that know thy name will put their trust in thee:
for thou, Lord, hast not forsaken them that seek thee.

Psalm 9:10

The Lord is my shepherd; I shall not want.

He maketh me to lie down in green pastures: he leadeth me beside the still waters.

He restoreth my soul: he leadeth me in the paths of
righteousness for his name's sake.

Yea, though I walk through the valley of the shadow of
death, I will fear no evil: for thou art with me; thy rod
and thy staff they comfort me.

Thou preparest a table before me in the presence of
mine enemies: thou anointest my head with oil; my cup
runneth over.

Surely goodness and mercy shall follow me all the
days of my life: and I will dwell in the house of the Lord
forever.

Psalm 23

I had fainted, unless I had believed to see the goodness of the Lord in the land of the living.

Psalm 27:13

Wait on the Lord: be of good courage, and he shall strengthen thine heart: wait, I say, on the Lord.

Psalm 27:14

O Lord my God, I cried unto thee, and thou hast healed me.

Psalm 30:2

I said, Lord, be merciful unto me: heal my soul; for I have sinned against thee.

Psalm 41:4

God is our refuge and strength, a very present help in trouble.

Psalm 46:1

Create in me a clean heart, O God; and renew a right spirit within me.

Psalm 51:10

The sacrifices of God are a broken spirit: a broken and contrite heart, O God, thou wilt not despise.

Psalm 51:17

Cast thy burden upon the Lord, and he shall sustain thee: he shall never suffer the righteous to be moved.

Psalm 55:22

My flesh and my heart faileth: but God is the strength of my heart, and my portion for ever.

Psalm 73:26

Because thou hast made the Lord, which is my refuge, even the Most High, thy habitation;
There shall no evil befall thee, neither shall any plague come nigh thy dwelling.

Psalm 91:9–10

Bless the Lord, O my soul, and forget not all his benefits:

Who forgiveth all thine iniquities; who healeth all thy diseases.

Psalm 103:2–3

I will lift up mine eyes unto the hills, from whence cometh my help.

My help cometh from the Lord, which made heaven and earth.

Psalm 121:1–2

My son, forget not my law; but let thine heart keep my commandments:

For length of days, and long life, and peace, shall they add to thee.

Let not mercy and truth forsake thee: bind them about thy neck; write them upon the table of thine heart:

So shalt thou find favor and good understanding in the sight of God and man.

Trust in the Lord with all thine heart; and lean not unto thine own understanding.

In all thy ways acknowledge him, and he shall direct thy paths.

Be not wise in thine own eyes: fear the Lord, and depart from evil.

Proverbs 3:1–7

My son, attend to my words; incline thine ear unto my sayings.

Let them not depart from thine eyes; keep them in the midst of thine heart.

For they are life unto those that find them, and health to all their flesh.

Proverbs 4:20–22

Keep thy heart with all diligence; for out of it are the issues of life.

Proverbs 4:23

He that is slow to anger is better than the mighty; and he that ruleth his spirit than he that taketh a city.

Proverbs 16:32

A merry heart doeth good like a medicine: but a broken spirit drieth the bones.

Proverbs 17:22

Surely he hath borne our griefs, and carried our sorrows: yet we did esteem him stricken, smitten of God, and afflicted.

But he was wounded for our transgressions, he was bruised for our iniquities: the chastisement of our peace was upon him; and with his stripes we are healed.

Isaiah 53:4–5

But the wicked are like the troubled sea, when it cannot rest, whose waters cast up mire and dirt.

There is no peace, saith my God, to the wicked.

Isaiah 57:20–21

The Spirit of the Lord God is upon me; because the Lord hath anointed me to preach good tidings unto the meek; he hath sent me to bind up the broken-hearted, to proclaim liberty to the captives, and the opening of the prison to them that are bound.

Isaiah 61:1

Heal me, O Lord, and I shall be healed; save me, and I shall be saved: for thou art my praise.

Jeremiah 17:14

For I will restore health unto thee, and I will heal thee of thy wounds, saith the Lord.

Jeremiah 30:17

I will bind up that which was broken, and will strengthen that which was sick.

Ezekiel 34:16

A new heart also will I give you, and a new spirit will I put within you: and I will take away the stony heart out of your flesh, and I will give you a heart of flesh.

Ezekiel 36:26

Thus saith the Lord God unto these bones; Behold, I will cause breath to enter into you, and ye shall live.

Ezekiel 37:5

The Lord is good, a stronghold in the day of trouble; and he knoweth them that trust in him.

Nahum 1:7

And as thou hast believed, so be it done unto thee.

Matthew 8:13

According to your faith be it unto you.

Matthew 9:29

And besought him that they might only touch the hem of his garment: and as many as touched were made perfectly whole.

Matthew 14:36

And great multitudes came unto him, having with them those that were lame, blind, dumb, maimed, and many others, and cast them down at Jesus' feet; and he healed them.

Matthew 15:30

And great multitudes followed him; and he healed them there.

Matthew 19:2

And he healed many that were sick of divers diseases, and cast out many devils; and suffered not the devils to speak, because they knew him.

Mark 1:34

Thy faith hath made thee whole; go in peace, and be whole of thy plague.

Mark 5:34

And whithersoever he entered, into villages, or cities, or country, they laid the sick in the streets, and besought him that they might touch if it were but the border of his garment: and as many as touched him were made whole.

Mark 6:56

For what shall it profit a man, if he shall gain the whole world, and lose his own soul?

Mark 8:36

Go your way, and tell John what things ye have seen and heard; how that the blind see, the lame walk, the lepers are cleansed, the deaf hear, the dead are raised, to the poor the gospel is preached.

And blessed is he, whosoever shall not be offended in me.

Luke 7:22–23

For the Son of man is not come to destroy men's lives, but to save them.

Luke 9:56

In your patience possess ye your souls.

Luke 21:19

Father, if thou be willing, remove this cup from me; nevertheless, not my will, but thine, be done.

Luke 22:42

I am come that they might have life, and that they might have it more abundantly.

John 10:10

Now ye are clean through the word which I have spoken unto you.

John 15:3

These things I have spoken unto you, that in me ye might have peace. In the world ye shall have tribulation: but be of good cheer; I have overcome the world.

John 16:33

Peter said, Silver and gold have I none; but such as I have give I thee: In the name of Jesus Christ of Nazareth rise up and walk.

Acts 3:6

God anointed Jesus of Nazareth with the Holy Ghost and with power: who went about doing good, and healing all that were oppressed of the devil; for God was with him.

Acts 10:38

The Spirit also helpeth our infirmities: for we know not what we should pray for as we ought: but the Spirit itself maketh intercession for us with groanings which cannot be uttered.

And he that searcheth the hearts knoweth what is the mind of the Spirit, because he maketh intercession for the saints according to the will of God.

Romans 8:26–27

And be not conformed to this world: but be ye transformed by the renewing of your mind, that ye may prove what is that good, and acceptable, and perfect will of God.

Romans 12:2

Surely you know that you are God's temple, and that God's Spirit lives in you!

1 Corinthians 3:16 (TEV)

The letter killeth, but the spirit giveth life.

2 Corinthians 3:6

We are troubled on every side, yet not distressed; we are perplexed, but not in despair;

Persecuted, but not forsaken; cast down, but not destroyed.

2 Corinthians 4:8–9

For our light affliction, which is but for a moment, worketh for us a far more exceeding and eternal weight of glory.

2 Corinthians 4:17

Therefore if any man be in Christ, he is a new creature: old things are passed away; behold, all things are become new.

2 Corinthians 5:17

And God is able to make all grace abound toward you; that ye, always having all sufficiency in all things, may abound to every good work.

2 Corinthians 9:8

My grace is sufficient for thee: for my strength is made perfect in weakness.

2 Corinthians 12:9

This one thing I do, forgetting those things which are behind, and reaching forth unto those things which are before,

I press toward the mark for the prize of the high calling of God in Christ Jesus.

Philippians 3:13–14

Be careful for nothing; but in every thing by prayer and supplication with thanksgiving let your requests be made known unto God.

And the peace of God, which passeth all understanding, shall keep your hearts and minds through Christ Jesus.

Philippians 4:6–7

But the Lord is faithful, who shall stablish you, and keep you from evil.

2 Thessalonians 3:3

Wherefore lift up the hands which hang down, and the feeble knees.

Hebrews 12:12

For God hath not given us the spirit of fear; but of power, and of love, and of a sound mind.

2 Timothy 1:7

Blessed is the man that endureth temptation: for when he is tried, he shall receive the crown of life, which the Lord hath promised to them that love him.

James 1:12

Is any sick among you? let him call for the elders of the church; and let them pray over him, anointing him with oil in the name of the Lord:

And the prayer of faith shall save the sick, and the Lord shall raise him up; and if he have committed sins, they shall be forgiven him.

Confess your faults one to another, and pray one for another, that ye may be healed. The effectual fervent prayer of a righteous man availeth much.

James 5:14–16

But if we confess our sins to God, we can trust him, for he does what is right—he will forgive our sins and make us clean from all our wrongdoing.

1 John 1:9 (TEV)

Beloved, I wish above all things that thou mayest prosper and be in health, even as thy soul prospereth.

3 John 2

Eight
The Cure for Sorrow

————————

*And I heard a great voice out of heaven
saying, Behold, the tabernacle of God is
with men, and he will dwell with them,
and they shall be his people, and God
himself shall be with them,
and be their God.*

*And God shall wipe away all tears from
their eyes; and there shall be no more
death, neither sorrow, nor crying, neither
shall there be any more pain: for the
former things are passed away.*

*And he that sat upon the throne said,
Behold, I make all things new. And he said
unto me, Write: for these words
are true and faithful.*

Revelation 21:3–5

In this world there is so much trouble, so much pain, sorrow, and death. Those who believe in Jesus Christ have a tremendous victory promised them. And this victory comes because we are his and he is ours.

So great is his love that he dries away human tears. No more shall there be death and crying. What a promise! By his vast power, death itself is overcome. Everything becomes gloriously new.

This is perhaps the great and ultimate truth, that in Christ and God, everything, both in persons and in the world, is changed; all becomes fresh and new and transformed.

Thus, the final glorious promise of God's goodness is the triumph of his love over pain and death.

Whoever embarks upon the Christian life will have periods of testing. However strong our faith, we will experience "down" moments. We may see the things we believe in flouted. It may seem that Satan, not God, controls human affairs. We will not be spared opposition. We will be criticized, mistreated, misunderstood. The way will be far from easy.

When such times come, fall further back on God, pray more earnestly, surrender more completely.

Certain things are inevitable for each of us in life, and death is one of them. We all share it. But you can emerge from your sorrow stronger and more mature, if you have faith and courage. It will help to look for opportunities to give comfort and love to other people. By helping to relieve the sorrow of others, your own will become easier to bear.

God will comfort your heart. The Christian message gives us this glorious hope. Death is not the end of life but only the beginning.

The physical body, the mortal house that your soul, the real you, uses as you live and work in this world will, like all material substances, gradually wear out.

Then you will move into another "house" in which the laws of materiality do not operate. Thus we have much to look forward to. Following God's laws, we are building now our spiritual "house" for eternity.

When we believe and ask for pardon, it will be granted. When our hearts accept him, Christ admits us to paradise.

Now therefore fear ye not: I will nourish you, and your little ones. And he comforted them.

Genesis 50:21

Forgive thy people that have sinned against thee, and all their transgressions wherein they have transgressed against thee, and give them compassion.

1 Kings 8:50

For I know that my Redeemer liveth, and that he shall stand at the latter day upon the earth.

Job 19:25

Weeping may endure for a night, but joy cometh in the morning.

Psalm 30:5

The Lord is nigh unto them that are of a broken heart; and saveth such as be of a contrite spirit.

Psalm 34:18

Thou shalt guide me with thy counsel, and afterward receive me to glory.

Psalm 73:24

For the Lord God is a sun and shield: the Lord will give grace and glory: no good thing will he withhold from them that walk uprightly.

Psalm 84:11

For thou, Lord, art good, and ready to forgive; and plenteous in mercy unto all them that call upon thee.

Psalm 86:5

For he shall give his angels charge over thee, to keep thee in all thy ways.

Psalm 91:11

Make a joyful noise unto the Lord, all ye lands.

Serve the Lord with gladness: come before his presence with singing.

Know ye that the Lord he is God: it is he that hath made us, and not we ourselves; we are his people, and the sheep of his pasture.

Enter into his gates with thanksgiving, and into his courts with praise: be thankful unto him, and bless his name.

For the Lord is good; his mercy is everlasting; and his truth endureth to all generations.

Psalm 100

As far as the east is from the west, so far hath he removed our transgressions from us.

Like as a father pitieth his children, so the Lord pitieth them that fear him.

For he knoweth our frame; he remembereth that we are dust. . . .

But the mercy of the Lord is from everlasting to everlasting.

Psalm 103:12–14, 17

O praise the Lord, all ye nations: praise him, all ye people.

For his merciful kindness is great toward us: and the truth of the Lord endureth for ever. Praise ye the Lord.

Psalm 117

It is vain for you to rise up early, to sit up late, to eat the bread of sorrows: for so he giveth his beloved sleep.

Psalm 127:2

But there is forgiveness with thee, that thou mayest be feared.

Psalm 130:4

Hope in the Lord: for with the Lord there is mercy.

Psalm 130:7

Though I walk in the midst of trouble, thou wilt revive me: thou shalt stretch forth thine hand against the wrath of mine enemies, and thy right hand shall save me.

The Lord will perfect that which concerneth me: thy mercy, O Lord, endureth for ever: forsake not the works of thine own hands.

Psalm 138:7–8

Search me, O God, and know my heart: try me, and know my thoughts:

And see if there be any wicked way in me, and lead me in the way everlasting.

Psalm 139:23–24

To every thing there is a season, and a time to every purpose under the heaven:

A time to be born, and a time to die; a time to plant, and a time to pluck up that which is planted;

A time to kill, and a time to heal; a time to break down, and a time to build up;

A time to weep, and a time to laugh; a time to mourn, and a time to dance;

A time to cast away stones, and a time to gather stones together; a time to embrace, and a time to refrain from embracing;

A time to get, and a time to lose; a time to keep, and a time to cast away;

A time to rend, and a time to sew; a time to keep silence, and a time to speak;

A time to love, and a time to hate; a time of war, and a time of peace.

Ecclesiastes 3:1–8

The Lord is good, a stronghold in the day of trouble; and he knoweth them that trust in him.

Nahum 1:7

Fear not them which kill the body, but are not able to kill the soul: but rather fear him which is able to destroy both soul and body in hell.

Are not two sparrows sold for a farthing? and one of them shall not fall on the ground without your Father.

But the very hairs of your head are all numbered.

Fear ye not therefore, ye are of more value than many sparrows.

Matthew 10:28–31

But he that shall endure unto the end, the same shall be saved.

Matthew 24:13

Lo, I am with you alway, even unto the end of the world.

Matthew 28:20

And he said unto Jesus, Lord, remember me when thou comest into thy kingdom.

And Jesus said unto him, Verily I say unto thee, To-day shalt thou be with me in paradise.

Luke 23:42–43

Let not your heart be troubled: ye believe in God, believe also in me.

In my Father's house, are many mansions: if it were not so, I would have told you. I go to prepare a place for you.

And if I go and prepare a place for you, I will come again, and receive you unto myself; that where I am, there ye may be also.

John 14:1–3

Yet a little while, and the world seeth me no more; but ye see me: because I live, ye shall live also.

John 14:19

Verily, verily, I say unto you, That ye shall weep and lament, but the world shall rejoice; and ye shall be sorrowful, but your sorrow shall be turned into joy. . . .

And ye now therefore have sorrow: but I will see you again, and your heart shall rejoice, and your joy no man taketh from you.

John 16:20, 22

Because he hath appointed a day, in the which he will judge the world in righteousness by that man whom he hath ordained; whereof he hath given asurance unto all men, in that he hath raised him from the dead.

Acts 17:31

For the wages of sin is death; but the gift of God is eternal life through Jesus Christ our Lord.

Romans 6:23

O wretched man that I am! who shall deliver me from the body of this death?

I thank God through Jesus Christ our Lord.

Romans 7:24–25

In all these things we are more than conquerors through him that loved us.

For I am persuaded, that neither death, nor life, nor angels, nor principalities, nor powers, nor things present, nor things to come,

Nor height, nor depth, nor any other creature, shall be able to separate us from the love of God, which is in Christ Jesus our Lord.

Romans 8:37–39

Eye hath not seen, nor ear heard, neither have entered into the heart of man, the things which God hath prepared for them that love him.

1 Corinthians 2:9

This corruptible must put on incorruption, and this mortal must put on immortality.

So when this corruptible shall have put on incorruption, and this mortal shall have put on immortality, then shall be brought to pass the saying that is written, Death is swallowed up in victory.

O death, where is thy sting? O grave, where is thy victory?

1 Corinthians 15:53–55

Blessed be God, . . . the God of all comfort;

Who comforteth us in all our tribulation, that we may be able to comfort them which are in any trouble, by the comfort wherewith we ourselves are comforted of God.

2 Corinthians 1:3–4

145

For we know that if our earthly house of this tabernacle were dissolved, we have a building of God, an house not made with hands, eternal in the heavens.

2 Corinthians 5:1

We are confident, I say, and willing rather to be absent from the body, and to be present with the Lord.

2 Corinthians 5:8

Be not deceived; God is not mocked: for whatsoever a man soweth, that shall he also reap.

For he that soweth to his flesh shall of the flesh reap corruption; but he that soweth to the Spirit shall of the Spirit reap life everlasting.

Galatians 6:7, 8

According to my earnest expectation and my hope, that in nothing I shall be ashamed, but that with all boldness, as always, so now also Christ shall be magnified in my body, whether it be by life, or by death.

For to me to live is Christ, and to die is gain.

Philippians 1:20–21

But I would not have you to be ignorant, brethren, concerning them which are asleep, that ye sorrow not, even as others which have no hope.

For if we believe that Jesus died and rose again, even so them also which sleep in Jesus will God bring with him.

For this we say unto you by the word of the Lord, that we which are alive and remain unto the coming of the Lord shall not prevent them which are asleep.

For the Lord himself shall descend from heaven with a shout, with the voice of the archangel, and with the trump of God: and the dead in Christ shall rise first:

Then we which are alive and remain shall be caught up together with them in the clouds, to meet the Lord in the air: and so shall we ever be with the Lord.

Wherefore comfort one another with these words.

1 Thessalonians 4:13–18

Fight the good fight of faith, lay hold on eternal life, whereunto thou art also called, and hast professed a good profession before many witnesses.

1 Timothy 6:12

Laying up in store for themselves a good foundation against the time to come, that they may lay hold on eternal life.

1 Timothy 6:19

In hope of eternal life, which God, that cannot lie, promised before the world began.

Titus 1:2

But we see Jesus, who was made a little lower than the angels for the suffering of death, crowned with glory and honor; that he by the grace of God should taste death for every man.

Hebrews 2:9

They shall hunger no more, neither thirst any more; neither shall the sun light on them, nor any heat.

For the Lamb which is in the midst of the throne shall feed them, and shall lead them unto living fountains of waters: and God shall wipe away all tears from their eyes.

Revelation 7:16–17